Attempt Great Things for God

DAG HEWARD-MILLS

Parchment House

ATTEMPT GREAT THINGS FOR GOD

Copyright © 2018 Dag Heward-Mills

First Edition published by Parchment House 2019
1st Printing 2019

Find out more about Dag Heward-Mills
Healing Jesus Crusade
Write to: evangelist@daghewardmills.org
Website: www.daghewardmills.org
Facebook: Dag Heward-Mills
Twitter: @EvangelistDag

ISBN: 978-1-64329-208-3

Contents

CHAPTER 1

Attempt Great Things

Enlarge the place of thy tent, and let them stretch forth the curtains of thine habitations: spare not, lengthen thy cords, and strengthen thy stakes;

Isaiah 54:2

This book is about attempting to do something great for God. You will discover many great things you can do for the Lord. A great thing is something that God calls great. In this book we are interested in things that are great in the eyes of God. We are interested in things that are called "great" in the Bible. What is great to a businessman may not be great to a servant of God. What is called "great" to a politician may not be called "great" in the sight of God.

These words from the prophet Isaiah are telling us to attempt to create a larger tent. Attempt to build a bigger tent. Expect more people to occupy the tent. Expect to need a bigger tent to give a covering to a larger crowd.

The prophecy is clear for all who are interested in the visions of God. The visions of God tell us to enlarge our ministries. The visions of God tell us to expect great things and to attempt great things.

William Carey, the great missionary to India, is the one who coined these famous words, "Attempt Great things for God and expect great things for God." The prophet gave the command to enlarge the tent and lengthen its cords. Why is that? Why would you have to enlarge the tent? Because you are expecting great things!

It is important for Christians to expect great things from God and to attempt great things for God. It is sad to say that many believers are not attempting great things for God. Instead of attempting great things for God, people are being side-tracked into business schemes and other ventures. Greater things can be done for the Lord.

And he said unto them, ye are they which justify yourselves before men; but God knoweth your hearts: FOR THAT WHICH IS HIGHLY ESTEEMED AMONG MEN IS ABOMINATION IN THE SIGHT OF GOD.

Luke 16:15

Every time you do great secular things, you reduce your chances of doing great things for God. Great things on earth are not great things for God. Earthly things have left the church dry. That which is highly esteemed among men is an abomination in the sight of God!

Many have set the visions of heaven and of God aside. Instead of seeing that we can do great things for God, church leaders have led the church into business, education and other secular social works.

Soul winning and church planting are not the same as building secular schools and health institutions. Salvation is a very spiritual thing. A church is a very spiritual body. A church is not a building. Salvation is not education. Salvation is the conversion of the soul and the transformation of the spirit of a man. Making disciples for Jesus is not the same as raising leaders and entrepreneurs for the business world. When I speak about attempting great things for God, I am not talking about building hotels, universities, secondary schools, boreholes and connecting electricity to villages. I am talking about achieving the goal for which Jesus Christ came into this world; the salvation of this world through the blood of Jesus Christ! The greatest work is indeed a spiritual work.

Dear Christian leader, please stop misleading the church! Stop making us think that creating earthly monuments, building human institutions, doing business, engaging in politics is the same as doing the great works of God.

Let's get it straight! No one else can do what the church does. No university can preach the gospel. No university plants churches! No secondary school ministers Holy Spirit baptism or prays for the sick. No hospital is charged with the preaching of Jesus Christ the same yesterday, today and forever. No hotel or business can do what a church does. A hotel is not a church!

When I speak of attempting great things for God, I am talking about fulfilling the Great Commission. I am talking about the original God-given mandate of the church to "Go into all the world and preach the gospel". We are not to preach physics, chemistry, biology, sociology or politics. We are to preach Jesus Christ and Him crucified! Most universities set aside the church and minimize its importance. It is amazing that the churches, which have been set aside and disregarded by the universities, are the very ones that set aside their own doctrine to follow the university's curriculum. Why does the church set aside the Bible and teach business, psychology, political science and business management in the pulpit. Why doesn't the university set aside its business studies, psychology, political science and business management and teach the Bible in its classrooms?

Let us attempt great things for God! Let us win souls for Jesus! Let us build churches for God! Let us do the things the bibleBible says are great works. Let us focus on spiritual things that have eternal value. Let us not be impressed with earthly glamour. The things that are highly esteemed among men are an abomination before God. These are the words of Jesus.

CHAPTER 2

Attempt Great Exploits

Then shall he return into his land with great riches; and his heart shall be against the holy covenant; and he shall do exploits, and return to his own land. At the time appointed he shall return, and come toward the south; but it shall not be as the former, or as the latter. For the ships of Chittim shall come against him: therefore he shall be grieved, and return, and have indignation against the holy covenant: so shall he do; he shall even return, and have intelligence with them that forsake the holy covenant. And arms shall stand on his part, and they shall pollute the sanctuary of strength, and shall take away the daily sacrifice, and they shall place the abomination that maketh desolate. And such as do wickedly against the covenant shall he corrupt by flatteries: but THE PEOPLE THAT DO KNOW THEIR GOD SHALL BE STRONG, AND DO EXPLOITS. And they that understand among the people shall instruct many: yet they shall fall by the sword, and by flame, by captivity, and by spoil, many days.

Daniel 11:28-33

What Are Exploits?

Exploits are the works of God! An exploit is a notable achievement! Exploits are striking accomplishments! Exploits are bold undertakings! Exploits are daring feats! An exploit is a brilliant and a heroic feat! Exploits are the works of the Father! Exploits are the works of Jesus! Exploits are preaching the word of God like Jesus did. Exploits are having miracles, signs and wonders. Exploits are building churches for Jesus. Exploits are doing the will of God.

Exploits are necessary to validate your calling. There is a lot of talk today. People say many things and speak many great words. In the end, there is very little fruit in spite of all the plenty talk. But exploits differentiate fruit-bearers from noisemakers! Exploits tell us whom we should listen to and whom we should follow. Exploits tell us who the genuine ministers are. Jesus always encouraged people to believe in Him because of His works. He told the people that His works were speaking for Him.

Many people say they are called. In the end, only a few are chosen! Many people claim that God has sent them. But why is it that so few end up doing something for the Lord? Talk is cheap!

It is easy to say you are called but can you overcome the obstacles to your calling? It is not what you say that matters. What have you been through? What have you survived? What have you overcome? A man of exploits has overcome many things. A man of exploits has survived many things.

I want you to become a man of exploits. Do not talk too much at meetings. Have you noticed that people who talk a lot in movies often get shot? Often, when they are supposed to eliminate the enemy, they talk a lot, threatening and goading over their enemy. Too much talk is dangerous! Get down to the job and do exploits for Jesus!

In these last days, we need doers, not talkers! In these last days we need men who are going to do exploits for Jesus. Those that know their God will do exploits (Daniel 11:32). Exploits are indeed a sign of people who are deep in God. People who are strong do exploits. People who are real do exploits! People who are made up of steel do exploits. Reeds shaking in the wind do not accomplish anything for God. Men of straw do not accomplish exploits. Men who are pushed around by the wind do nothing for God. Men who are pushed around by their wives do nothing for God. People who are pushed around by circumstances cannot bear fruit. John the Baptist could not be shaken with the wind. John the Baptist did not live delicately in the king's court. He was a hard man! He was resistant to pressure! He was on a mission! He was there to do exploits!

> And when the messengers of John were departed, he began to speak unto the people concerning John, What went ye out into the wilderness for to see? A reed shaken with the wind? But what went ye out for to see? A man clothed in soft raiment? Behold, they which are gorgeously apparelled, and live delicately, are in kings' courts. But what went ye out for to see? A prophet? Yea, I say unto you, and much more than a prophet.
>
> Luke 7:24-26

A person who has attempted exploits has overcome excuses and reasons why things cannot be done. Many people are neutralised by circumstances. Do not come up with excuses to kill your calling. Do not come up with plenty excuses that wipe out the exploits that you are supposed to do. Do exploits instead of coming up with excuses. John the Baptist did not give the wind as an excuse. He was simply not shaken by the wind.

The Power of Exploits

1.   Exploits are a sign of the strength that you carry.

And such as do wickedly against the covenant shall he corrupt by flatteries: but the people that do know their God SHALL BE STRONG, AND DO EXPLOITS.

Daniel 11:32

Be a man of strength! Do not be a weakling! Rise up and demonstrate your strength in God. Exploits are not given to weaklings! God has a call for you to do exploits! The people who know their God will be strong and do exploits.

2. Exploits are a sign of how much you know God.

And such as do wickedly against the covenant shall he corrupt by flatteries: BUT THE PEOPLE THAT DO KNOW THEIR GOD shall be strong, and DO EXPLOITS.

Daniel 11:32

Many people do not know God. They know *about* God and they have read the Bible. But they do not know God. Knowing God is essential for bearing fruits. Go deeper and get to know God and you will do exploits.

3. Exploits are works that make people believe in you!

Believe me that I am in the Father, and the Father in me: or else BELIEVE ME FOR THE VERY WORKS' SAKE.

John 14:11

Jesus taught us to believe in people who do exploits. You may wonder why no one believes in your calling or no one reads your books. Your words are not what matter. It is the works that you do! Believe me for the very works' sake! I have learnt not to trust in people just because of their great messages. One day, I saw a man speaking great words of wisdom on television. He was so impressive that people all over the world were tuning in and commenting on his message. But I found it difficult to listen to his preaching. This man had no great works behind him. Although he had been a preacher for many years and had thousands of dollars running through his hands, he had not been able to build anything. He had no church building but was still renting public halls for his church. Through wisdom a house is built (Proverbs 24:3). The wisdom of God results in mighty works. What wisdom is this that such mighty works are wrought by the hand of Jesus? (Mark 6:2) The wisdom of Jesus resulted in mighty works.

Jesus asked us to believe in Him because of His works. Always look for works and not words! It is not my idea that you should assess people through their works. Jesus taught us that it was a good way to determine whom to believe in. Gravitate towards those who have works to support what they say. People must have works to support their wisdom!

4. **Exploits are works that make people believe that God is in you.**

If I do not the works of my Father, believe me not. But if I do, though ye believe not me, believe the works: that ye may know, and BELIEVE, THAT THE FATHER IS IN ME, AND I IN HIM.

John 10:37-38

We are all scared of following a man. When we go to church, we want to see God and we want to experience Him in His fullness. No one wants a man. Everyone wants God! Exploits make people realise that God is with you. Like Nicodemus said, "No one can do these things except God is with him" (John 3:2). It is only the presence of God that we seek. One of the ways to know that God is with a person are the exploits he does. If God was not present, the exploits would not be done.

5. **Exploits show God's approval of you and your calling.**

Ye men of Israel, hear these words; Jesus of Nazareth, A MAN APPROVED OF GOD AMONG YOU BY MIRACLES AND WONDERS AND SIGNS, which God did by him in the midst of you, as ye yourselves also know:

Acts 2:22

In the world today, there is very little a person can do that shows that God is with him. Human beings cannot do miracles, signs and wonders. Only God can heal a person. When there are signs and wonders, it is evidence that God is approving of a person. Exploits must begin to take place in your life and ministry. It is a sign of God's approval of you and your ministry.

6. Exploits help you to preach the gospel.

And he said unto them, go ye into all the world, and preach the gospel to every creature. He that believeth and is baptized shall be saved; but he that believeth not shall be damned. And these signs shall follow them that believe; In my name shall they cast out devils; they shall speak with new tongues; they shall take up serpents; and if they drink any deadly thing, it shall not hurt them; they shall lay hands on the sick, and they shall recover.

Mark 16:15-18

Miracles, signs and wonders are exploits. These exploits definitely help you to preach the gospel. There are many holy books in the world today. There are many famous prophets in the world today. There are many who claim to be saviours of the world. What shows that the Bible is the real holy book? What shows that Jesus is the Son of God? Exploits! You must do exploits in the ministry. You must have miracles, signs and wonders in your ministry.

7. Exploits make people recognize you and honour you.

And there they preached the gospel. And there sat a certain man at Lystra, impotent in his feet, being a cripple from his mother's womb, who never had walked: The same heard Paul speak: who stedfastly beholding him, and perceiving that he had faith to be healed, Said with a loud voice, Stand upright on thy feet. And he leaped and walked. And when the people saw what Paul had done, they lifted up their voices, saying in the speech of Lycaonia, The gods are come down to us in the likeness of men. And they called Barnabas, Jupiter; and Paul, Mercurius, because he was the chief speaker. THEN THE PRIEST OF JUPITER, WHICH WAS BEFORE THEIR CITY, BROUGHT OXEN AND GARLANDS UNTO THE GATES, AND WOULD HAVE

DONE SACRIFICE WITH THE PEOPLE. Which when the apostles, Barnabas and Paul, heard of, they rent their clothes, and ran in among the people, crying out, And saying, Sirs, why do ye these things? We also are men of like passions with you, and preach unto you that ye should turn from these vanities unto the living God, which made heaven, and earth, and the sea, and all things that are therein: Who in times past suffered all nations to walk in their own ways.

Acts 14:7-16

Perhaps you are not recognized or appreciated in your life and ministry. Initially, Apostle Paul was ignored when he came to Lystra. After one miracle, everything changed. Paul was recognized and presented with oxen and garlands. This is what is going to happen to you in your ministry when you do exploits. You will be recognized and honoured through the exploits of your ministry.

CHAPTER 3

Attempt Great Things *for God* Not for Yourself

THE WORD THAT JEREMIAH THE PROPHET SPAKE UNTO BARUCH the son of Neriah, when he had written these words in a book at the mouth of Jeremiah, in the fourth year of Jehoiakim the son of Josiah king of Judah, saying, Thus saith the Lord, the God of Israel, unto thee, O Baruch; Thou didst say, Woe is me now! For the Lord hath added grief to my sorrow; I fainted in my sighing, and I find no rest. Thus shalt thou say unto him, The Lord saith thus; Behold, that which I have built will I break down, and that which I have planted I will pluck up, even this whole land. And SEEKEST THOU GREAT THINGS FOR THYSELF? SEEK THEM NOT: for, behold, I will bring evil upon all flesh, saith the Lord: but thy life will I give unto thee for a prey in all places whither thou goest.

Jeremiah 45:1-5

Baruch was a scribe who wrote down the prophecies and messages of Jeremiah. He was so close to Jeremiah that he became a target of the enemies of Jeremiah. God blessed Baruch with a personal prophecy. He told him, "Do not seek great things for yourself." There is no point in seeking great things for yourself because evil is coming upon the earth. That evil will destroy all the great accomplishments you have sought. "Seek them not" is the word to Baruch. I believe that is the word of God for all of us. Do not seek great things for yourself! Seek great things for God! As you seek great things for God, God will give you all the things you have not sought.

Your life can be spent seeking great things for yourself or seeking great things for God. You must decide to spend your life seeking great things for God and not for yourself.

Most people spend their lives seeking great things for themselves. I am sad to report that most people do not lay hold on the great things that they seek for. That is why it is great wisdom to attempt great things for God.

1. Jacob attempted great things for himself but was cheated out of greatness.

Unless God helps you, you cannot do much in this life. The Bible is full of examples of people who attempted great things for themselves. If God had not intervened, their lives would have amounted to nothing. That is the story of all men if God doesn't help them. There is so much corruption and cheating in the world that working hard doesn't yield very much for most people.

Why not choose to work hard for God and attempt great things for Him? Why live your life on this earth only to earn far less than you really deserve. When you work for God your rewards are in Heaven.

And Jacob was wroth, and chode with Laban: and Jacob answered and said to Laban, What is my trespass? What is my sin, that thou hast so hotly pursued after me? Whereas thou hast searched all my stuff, what hast thou found of all thy household stuff? Set it here before my brethren and thy brethren, that they may judge betwixt us both. This twenty years have I been with thee; thy ewes and thy she goats have not cast their young, and the rams of thy flock have I not eaten. That which was torn of beasts I brought not unto thee; I bare the loss of it; of my hand didst thou require it, whether stolen by day, or stolen by night. Thus I was; in the day the drought consumed me, and the frost by night; and my sleep departed from mine eyes. Thus have I been twenty years in thy house; I SERVED THEE FOURTEEN YEARS FOR THY TWO DAUGHTERS, AND SIX YEARS FOR THY CATTLE: AND THOU HAST CHANGED MY WAGES TEN TIMES. EXCEPT THE GOD OF MY FATHER, THE GOD OF ABRAHAM, AND THE FEAR OF ISAAC, HAD BEEN WITH ME, SURELY THOU HADST SENT ME AWAY NOW EMPTY. God hath seen mine affliction and the labour of my hands, and rebuked thee yesternight.

Genesis 31:36-42

2. Solomon attempted great things for himself but was disillusioned and disappointed.

Solomon built many things, houses, vineyards, orchard, pools, gardens and farms. Solomon built a temple and achieved earthly fame and wealth that no one ever has. He had no restrictions and acquired more wives than any known person. His great achievements brought him to the conclusion that everything achieved on this earth is useless and worthless. "All is vanity!" he said. Why bother to build great works which will be declared useless at the end of your life?

I MADE ME GREAT WORKS; I BUILDED ME HOUSES; I planted me vineyards: I made me gardens and orchards, and I planted trees in them of all kind of fruits: I made me pools of water, to water therewith the wood that bringeth forth trees: I got me servants and maidens, and had servants born in my house; also I had great possessions of great and small cattle above all that were in Jerusalem before me: I gathered me also silver and gold, and the

14

peculiar treasure of kings and of the provinces: I gat me men singers and women singers, and the delights of the sons of men, as musical instruments, and that of all sorts.

So I was great, and increased more than all that were before me in Jerusalem: also my wisdom remained with me. And whatsoever mine eyes desired I kept not from them, I withheld not my heart from any joy; for my heart rejoiced in all my labour: and this was my portion of all my labour. THEN I LOOKED ON ALL THE WORKS THAT MY HANDS HAD WROUGHT, AND ON THE LABOUR THAT I HAD LABOURED TO DO: AND, BEHOLD, ALL WAS VANITY AND VEXATION OF SPIRIT, AND THERE WAS NO PROFIT UNDER THE SUN.

Ecclesiastes 2:4-11

3. **The rich fool attempted great things for himself but was called out of this world before he could enjoy them.**

Attempting great things for yourself when you are not rich towards God will only lead to a sudden shock on the day of Judgement. Life on this earth is only the beginning of your real life. Life continues in eternity. Focusing only on earthly achievements is a big mistake. The rich fool found out to his amazement that God withdraws people without notice.

And he spake a parable unto them, saying, the ground of a certain rich man brought forth plentifully: And he thought within himself, saying, What shall I do, because I have no room where to bestow my fruits? And he said, this will I do: I WILL PULL DOWN MY BARNS, AND BUILD GREATER; and there will I bestow all my fruits and my goods. And I will say to my soul, Soul, thou hast much goods laid up for many years; take thine ease, eat, drink, and be merry. But God said unto him, Thou fool, this night thy soul shall be required of thee: then whose shall those things be, which thou hast provided? So is he that layeth up treasure for himself, and is not rich toward God.

Luke 12:16-21

4. **The rich young ruler attempted great things for himself but those things kept him away from God.** Don't waste your life acquiring great possessions that will keep you away from God. Attempt great things for God and He will give you great possessions if He wants to. What shall it profit a man if he gains the whole world and loses his soul? (Mark 8:36)

And he said unto him, Why callest thou me good? There is none good but one, that is, God: but if thou wilt enter into life, keep the commandments. He saith unto him, which? Jesus said, Thou shalt do no murder, Thou shalt not commit adultery, Thou shalt not steal, Thou shalt not bear false witness, Honour thy father and thy mother: and, Thou shalt love thy neighbour as thyself. The young man saith unto him, all these things have I kept from my youth up: what lack I yet? Jesus said unto him, If thou wilt be perfect, go and sell that thou hast, and give to the poor, and thou shalt have treasure in heaven: and come and follow me. But when the young man heard that saying, he went away sorrowful: FOR HE HAD GREAT POSSESSIONS. THEN SAID JESUS UNTO HIS DISCIPLES, VERILY I SAY UNTO YOU, THAT A RICH MAN SHALL HARDLY ENTER INTO THE KINGDOM OF HEAVEN. And again I say unto you, it is easier for a camel to go through the eye of a needle, than for a rich man to enter into the kingdom of God.

Matthew 19:17-24

5. **The Gentiles seek great things for themselves.**

Jesus never sought great things for Himself. Jesus taught us to seek great things for the kingdom of God. The reason why Jesus taught us to seek great things for the kingdom was to differentiate us from those who do not have faith in God. Your faith in God will lead you to seek great things for God. Big faith in God results in great achievements for God! Little faith results in little achievements for God! Seek ye first the kingdom of God. Believe that the kingdom of God is worthy of your life. Believe that seeking the kingdom of God is the greatest thing you can do. That is what will result in the greatest achievements.

Therefore take no thought, saying, what shall we eat? Or, what shall we drink? Or, wherewithal shall we be clothed? (For after all these things do the Gentiles seek:) for your heavenly Father knoweth that ye have need of all these things. But seek ye first the kingdom of God, and his righteousness; and all these things shall be added unto you. Take therefore no thought for the morrow: for the morrow shall take thought for the things of itself. Sufficient unto the day is the evil thereof.

Matthew 6:31-34

CHAPTER 4

Attempt Greater Works

Verily, verily, I say unto you, He that believeth on me, the works that I do shall he do also; and GREATER WORKS THAN THESE SHALL HE DO; because I go unto my Father.

John 14:12

The works that Jesus did are the standard for the works that we are to accomplish. We look at Jesus and His accomplishments and try to emulate Him. The Bible should be the basis for all our ideas. It is not enough to just come up with good ideas. Jesus gave a great prophecy of how we would do greater works. Jesus did great works and He prophesied that we would do even greater works. The great things we are to attempt are the things that Jesus did.

Today, people are doing great businesses, building harbours, banks, consultancies, factories, and hotels. Many are also building hospitals, building schools and universities, making boreholes, connecting electricity and providing housing for the aged. All these are great works indeed. But are they the great works that Jesus did?

It is easy to go astray while serving God. It is easy to do many different things and call them great works. However, when we get to heaven, we may want to grind them into powder so that their vanity and worthlessness does not appear before the host of heaven.

And Jesus went about all the cities and villages, TEACHING in their synagogues, and PREACHING the gospel of the kingdom, and HEALING every sickness and every disease among the people.

Matthew 9:35

Attempting great things is to do the greater works that Jesus prophesied about. Attempt to fulfil a great prophecy. Attempt great things for God by attempting to do the works that Jesus did and even more. Jesus Christ did great works and He prophesied that you would do even greater works. The works that Jesus did consisted of preaching, teaching and healing. Jesus travelled from place to place and showed compassion to many people. These are the great works that Jesus did.

Attempting great things for God is to at least do the works that Jesus did and then try to do more.

> **But I fear, lest by any means, as the serpent beguiled Eve through his subtilty, so your minds should be corrupted from the SIMPLICITY THAT IS IN CHRIST.**
>
> **2 Corinthians 11:3**

Do not be fooled by great men of God who are doing business, politics, education, medicine, investments, motivational preaching, secular lectures and humanitarian work. These are all good things. But the works of Jesus were simple: preaching, teaching and healing! Satan is crafty and he would love to beguile the church to turn away from the simplicity that is in Christ. Perhaps, the preaching of the gospel is too simple for many preachers. Indeed, the gospel is not too simple or too basic for us. It is we who have backslidden from the simplicity that is in Christ. The simplicity of the gospel is that Jesus died to save the world. The simplicity of Christ is that the blood of Jesus has been shed for every soul in this world. That is the simple message we are called out to teach. Many men of God have been beguiled by satan into preaching everything else but the simple pure gospel.

One day, I met a man of God who had given himself to "developing businesses, empowering people to become millionaires, affecting nations and having Christians in the market place". I was surprised that at the end of his life and ministry, he was emphasizing the need to plant churches. He had turned around and come back to the simplicity of the gospel. Why on earth do we claim to be making people into millionaires and developing businesses? Have these so-called millionaires and businessmen helped the church in any way? Most of the church has been emphasizing on these mysterious financial and secular goals for a long time. Meanwhile, we see no real church planting, no crusades, no evangelism and no expansion of the kingdom of God. Many towns and cities in the world are bereft of any new church plants planting activities or evangelistic activities.

Satan has indeed beguiled ministers of God to move away from the simplicity of the gospel to these high-sounding secular activities. These high-sounding goals may be lauded by the secular world but they are nothing but trash when put by the side of the cross of Jesus Christ. The development of businesses, the development of investments, the rise of motivational preaching and the delusion of market place message do not save people. People are saved when they are washed by the blood of Jesus.

God sent His Son to be Saviour of the world. Jesus came to save us from our sins. Jesus did not come to save this world from its financial confusion. The gospel must be preached! New churches must be planted! People must be saved! People must be born again! The cross of Jesus and the sacrifice of Jesus is the reason for the church. It must be popular again. Nonsense must be thrown out of the church! Christianity must become what it really is. A blood-washing, soul-saving religion!

CHAPTER 5

Attempt New Things

Moreover the word of the Lord came unto Jeremiah the second time, while he was yet shut up in the court of the prison, saying, Thus saith the Lord the maker thereof, the Lord that formed it, to establish it; the Lord is his name; Call unto me, and I will answer thee, and SHEW THEE GREAT AND MIGHTY THINGS, WHICH THOU KNOWEST NOT.

Jeremiah 33:1-3

Be open to do great and mighty things that God will show you in your lifetime. God will reveal great things as you walk along with Him. God does not show you all His plans in a day. They unfold bit by bit. A little here and a little there! Be open for new things! God has great things that He will show you. Do not get tired of attempting new things for God. When you are tired of attempting new things, you are tired of living.

There will never be a time that God will be silent towards you. He will always have a word, a direction and a message for you. The silence you are experiencing from God is because you have not obeyed the most recent instruction. When you get to the job of obeying His will for your life, you will hear him speak again.

When Paul was called to the ministry, he was told, "I will shew him how great things he must suffer for my name's sake" (Acts 9:16). God will be showing you things as you go along!

How to Discover the New Things

1. Be open to new books.

And Hilkiah the high priest said unto Shaphan the scribe, I HAVE FOUND THE BOOK of the law in the house of the Lord. And Hilkiah gave the book to Shaphan, and he read it . . .

Go ye, enquire of the Lord for me, and for the people, and for all Judah, concerning the words of this book that is found: for great is the wrath of the Lord that is kindled against us, because our fathers have not hearkened unto the words of this book, to do according unto all that which is written concerning us.

2 Kings 22:8, 13

Be open to great books and authors whose material you have never read before. Josiah, the king, was open to a new book that he discovered. This led to one of the greatest revivals in the history of Israel.

23

I am always searching for a book or an author whom God will use to bless me. I discovered Rick Joyner in a bookshop as I scanned through books trying to find something that would help my life and ministry. What a different it made in my life! Be open to new books and new authors whom you have never heard speak.

2. Be open to new men of God.

And the Syrians had gone out by companies, and had brought away captive out of the land of Israel a little maid; and she waited on Naaman's wife. And she said unto her mistress, Would God my lord were with THE PROPHET THAT IS IN SAMARIA! For he would recover him of his leprosy.

2 Kings 5:2-3

There are people who are doing great things and whom God is using. You may not have heard of them. In the days of Naaman the Syrian, there was a great prophet called Elisha. Naaman had not heard of Elisha. Naaman did not know that his life would change when he came in contact with Elisha.

When you have not encountered certain ministries, you would not know what God will do for you through them. The loudest ministries are found on television but they may not be the greatest. There are ministries that you must discover. They are part of God's plan for your life.

3. Be open to ancient ministries.

And he arose and went: and, behold, a man of Ethiopia, an eunuch of great authority under Candace queen of the Ethiopians, who had the charge of all her treasure, and had come to Jerusalem for to worship, Was returning, and SITTING IN HIS CHARIOT READ ESAIAS THE PROPHET.

Acts 8:27-28

The Ethiopian eunuch was open to the ancient ministry of Isaiah, the prophet. Isaiah the prophet lived hundreds of years before the Ethiopian eunuch lived. Yet, the Ethiopian eunuch was reading the prophet Isaiah's book. It is the searching through of the ancient ministry of Isaiah that brought salvation to the Ethiopian eunuch.

There are many things to learn from ministries that existed long ago. Today I learn from many ministers who are dead and gone. Indeed, there are many things to learn from ministers who lived two hundred years before you. In fact, I find that some of the purest messages can be found in ministries that existed many years ago.

Some of the messages that were preached in the past are not preached today. How would you ever hear the words of William Carey, Adoniram Judson or John Wesley if you are not open to ancient ministries?

There are precious people who once lived and ministered powerfully. Many people have forgotten what they stood for. Many people do not understand what they did. Their lives and their words will bless you beyond measure if you are open to them. God will do new things in your life if you are open to ancient ministries.

John Wesley lived a few hundred years ago, yet I admire him so much. I would like to achieve the many wonderful things that he did for God. I have read much about John Wesley's life. I have visited John Wesley's house, John Wesley's church and even his burial place. What a blessing that was to me! Opening myself up to this ancient ministry was definitely a turning point in my life.

4. Be open to travel.

Then after three years I went up to Jerusalem to see Peter, and abode with him fifteen days.

Galatians 1:18

Even though Paul had had a real revelation of Jesus Christ, he travelled to Jerusalem to see Apostle Peter. Be open to travel to meet men of God whom you have heard of. Paul had heard of Peter but he had not had a chance to have a deep interaction with him. If you do not travel, you will never meet certain men of God.

Travelling to Korea was once of the most important things I ever did. Travelling to Korea opened me up to David Yonggi Cho, who was the pastor of the largest church in the world at the time. That trip opened the door for me to fellowship with God's great servant. It also opened many doors of ministry for me. People who do not get up and go will never see certain things in their lives and ministry.

5. Be open to the power of God.

And it came to pass on a certain day, as he was teaching, that there were Pharisees and doctors of the law sitting by, which were come out of every town of Galilee, and Judaea, and Jerusalem: AND THE POWER OF THE LORD WAS PRESENT TO HEAL THEM.

Luke 5:17

The power of God was present when Jesus was teaching. People were sitting around casually but the power of God was present. When you are in the presence of a great person, always expect the power of God to be present. Expect to hear great things. Expect to hear short sentences and phrases that will change your life. Expect snippets that will revolutionise your entire existence.

I once had the privilege of being alone at dinner with a great man of God. I heard great words that became great keys to my ministry. This man of God asked me a very important question. Then he gave me one of the most important secrets for my ministry. Always expect the power of God to be present when you are in the presence of a great person. Expect to hear something that will change your life and ministry.

CHAPTER 6

Attempt to Love God

Then one of them, which was a lawyer, asked him a question, tempting him, and saying, Master, which is the GREAT COMMANDMENT in the law? Jesus said unto him, Thou shalt love the Lord thy God with all thy heart, and with all thy soul, and with all thy mind. This is the FIRST AND GREAT COMMANDMENT. And the second is like unto it, Thou shalt love thy neighbour as thyself. On these two commandments hang all the law and the prophets.

Matthew 22:35-40

The greatest commandment is to love God. Therefore, keeping this "great commandment" is a great accomplishment. It will definitely be a great achievement if you can keep the great commandment. The great commandment to all believers is to love the Lord with all our hearts and minds. It is indeed a great achievement to love God and as you read this chapter, you will see why it is a great thing to love God.

Seven Reasons Why it is a Great Achievement to Love God

1. Loving God is a great achievement because loving God is to love Someone you cannot see.

Think about the people you can see and how difficult it is to love them. It is not easy to love people. The break-up of relationships is proof of how difficult it is to love and be loved. Aren't there people who claim that they love you but you really cannot feel their love?

Loving someone is not as easy as it may seem. If it is that difficult to love someone you can see, how much more difficult will it be to love someone you cannot see!

2. Loving God is a great achievement because loving God is to love Someone you cannot hear.

Can you imagine what it is like to love someone who does not speak a word back to you?

Think about people who say, "I love you." How difficult it is to maintain relationships with people who have said, "I love you". Loving God involves speaking to Someone who does not say a word back to you.

Many people do not maintain their relationships because they do not communicate enough. Speaking and communication are an important part of maintaining relationships. Can you imagine what it is like to love someone who does not communicate at all in word or in writing?

3. Loving God is a great achievement because loving God is to love Someone you cannot feel.

Loving someone often involves having nice feelings about that person. Most of the people who say, "I love you" and who desperately want to get married, are experiencing some kind of feeling. It is when these feelings wane that people break up their relationships. It is difficult to have feelings in relation to God. Can you imagine what it is like to love a God whom you cannot feel, touch or sense? This is why loving God is a great accomplishment.

4. Loving God is a great achievement because you cannot love God the way you love man.

How do you know when someone loves you? Perhaps they will say, "I love you." Perhaps they will send love notes, go for walks, send gifts, speak kindly to you, chat with you, say nice things, sing your praises, send flowers, send cards, comment on your clothes, comment on your hair, say how handsome or beautiful you are and so on. Unfortunately, you cannot go for walks with God. You cannot send Him love notes. You cannot comment on His hair. You cannot comment on His clothes or His looks. It is not easy to love God because you cannot love Him the way you love a man. Loving God is indeed a great accomplishment!

5. Loving God is a great accomplishment because God is great and you are nothing.

It is not easy to relate with a great person. It is not easy to chat with a great person. It is not easy to know what to say! How difficult it is to relate with the greatest person of all – almighty God! How could you even attempt to chat with almighty God who knows everything about everything?

It is not easy to maintain a discussion with almighty God. What is even more difficult is the silence that comes from the almighty God. Silence often makes you feel stupid! You may feel more and more uncomfortable and insignificant in the presence of a great person. Indeed, the greatness of God can be a stumbling block to your relationship with the Father.

6. Loving God is a great achievement because God is holy and you know you are not.

As we get closer to God, we sense unworthiness, wretchedness and corruption in ourselves. Anyone who has had an encounter with God will know how unworthy, wretched and sinful he is when he approaches God! Most of us feel unworthy and unlovable in the presence of God.

Relationships break down when one party always feels inferior. It is a very dangerous thing to have an inferiority complex. Saying "I love you" and many assurances do not work on people with an inferiority complex. To relate happily and love God properly, you must overcome the inferiority complex you have because of your sins. You must accept that you are forgiven. You must accept that everything in the past is washed away by the blood of Jesus.

Another obstacle in loving God is that you are always confessing sins that you know you will commit again. You keep going back to the same sins and it makes you wonder if God takes you seriously. Like Isaiah, you can only shout, "Woe is me, I am unclean, I am undone."

In the year that king Uzziah died I saw also the Lord sitting upon a throne, high and lifted up, and his train filled the temple. Above it stood the seraphims: each one had six wings; with twain he covered his face, and with twain he covered his feet, and with twain he did fly. And one cried unto another, and said, Holy, holy, holy, is the Lord of hosts: the whole earth is full of his glory. And the posts of the door moved at the voice of him that cried, and the house was filled with smoke.

THEN SAID I, WOE IS ME! FOR I AM UNDONE; BECAUSE I AM A MAN OF UNCLEAN LIPS, AND I

DWELL IN THE MIDST OF A PEOPLE OF UNCLEAN LIPS: for mine eyes have seen the King, the Lord of hosts.

Isaiah 6:1-5

7. Loving God is a great achievement because God's love language is obedience.

He that hath my commandments, and keepeth them, he it is that loveth me: and he that loveth me shall be loved of my Father, and I will love him, and will manifest myself to him.

John 14:21

To love God is to understand obedience and to flow in simple obedience towards Him. Can you imagine loving a woman who says to you, "If you love me, *obey me*?" Can you imagine a woman saying, "I do not want any love notes, flowers, cards or gifts! Just be obedient to me!" Most of us will find it difficult to love this woman. But that is exactly how God wants to be loved. God does not want your love walks, your flowers or your cards. God wants obedience! God wants obedience as a sign of your love. God's love language is obedience!

CHAPTER 7

Attempt to Fight for God

And I say also unto thee, that thou art Peter, and upon this rock I will build my church; and THE GATES OF HELL shall not prevail against it.

Matthew 16:18

Anyone who attempts to build the church of God must be ready for a fight. Building churches is warfare! Church growth is warfare! Church planting is warfare! The gates of hell are postured against the building of the church. All types of devils are released against the building of the church. Without the willingness to fight, you cannot build the church of God. It is only when Jesus spoke of building the church that He mentioned the gates of hell. The gates of hell are not mentioned anywhere else in the Bible. This should send alarm bells ringing into the hearts of anyone who wants to build the church.

Without a willingness to fight you cannot be involved in church building or church growth. Church planting only happens to those who are willing to go to war. Do you want to attempt great things for God? Do you want to attempt to fight for God? What a great thing that would be if you can help in fighting to build the church of God! Remember, you will be fighting directly against the gates of hell.

Fight the good fight of faith, lay hold on eternal life, whereunto thou art also called, and hast professed a good profession before many witnesses.

1 Timothy 6:12

When you are tired of fighting you are tired of living! When you are tired of fighting, get ready to stop work and die. Attempting great things is all about fighting for God, fighting for the church and fighting for the name of Jesus Christ.

Most of life is a fight to achieve something or a fight to overcome something. Decide that your fight will be a fight for God! Paul declared that he had a great conflict because of the souls at Colossae and the souls at Laodicea. A great conflict for a worthy cause is a great thing! A great conflict for souls is a good thing!

For I would that ye knew WHAT GREAT CONFLICT I HAVE FOR YOU, and for them at Laodicea, and for as many as have not seen my face in the flesh; That their hearts might be comforted, being knit together

in love, and unto all riches of the full assurance of understanding, to the acknowledgement of the mystery of God, and of the Father, and of Christ;

Colossians 2:1-2

There are people who want to look good and have a peaceful existence with no conflict at all. That is not possible if you want to attempt great things for God. Even if you do not want to fight, others will bring the fight to you. There are many good causes to fight for in Christ. Be ready for a great conflict!

Are you ready to fight to achieve great things for God? One of the tests for a minister is his ability to build the church of God. Building will really test your resolve to fight. Building will test your resolve to fight for money, to fight for legal permits, to fight for documents, to fight for the professionals to do their work, to fight the waste of money, to fight delays, to fight excuses, to fight enemies of the project and to fight the devil himself. The gates of hell open up against every church building and church growth project.

For the builders, everyone had his sword girded by his side, and so builded. And he that sounded the trumpet was by me. And I said unto the nobles, and to the rulers, and to the rest of the people, THE WORK IS GREAT AND LARGE, and we are separated upon the wall, one far from another.

Nehemiah 4:18-19

Nehemiah did not build the walls of Jerusalem without a fight. All the builders had a sword on their side, ready to fight off those who were opposing their project. Nehemiah attempted great things for God. He attempted to build a wall around Jerusalem. He attempted to rebuild the ruins of God's holy city. Nehemiah will always be remembered for attempting to rebuild the walls of Jerusalem. He may not have succeeded completely but he attempted to do great things for God and will be remembered in eternity for this great work.

Will you build for God? Will you attempt great things for God? Will you fight for God? Or will you just try to build your own mansions and personal properties? Will you build churches? Are you ready for a great fight as you attempt great things for God?

CHAPTER 8

Attempt Preaching and Teaching!

Behold also the ships, which though they be so great, and are driven of fierce winds, yet are they turned about with a very small helm, whithersoever the governor listeth. Even so the tongue is a little member, and BOASTETH GREAT THINGS. BEHOLD, HOW GREAT A MATTER A LITTLE FIRE KINDLETH!

James 3:4-5

Y ou can attempt great things for God by preaching and teaching. Speaking for God is the greatest thing you can do with your life. Learn how to speak the word of God! The greatest job on earth is preaching and teaching! God will use your tongue to kindle great matters for God.

1. **Attempt great things by attempting to lead people to salvation! You must lead many people to salvation through the sinner's prayer.**

That if thou shalt confess with thy mouth the Lord Jesus, and shalt believe in thine heart that God hath raised him from the dead, thou shalt be saved. For with the heart man believeth unto righteousness; and with the mouth confession is made unto salvation.

Romans 10:9-10

You can be saved from hell through the use of your tongue. If you believe with your heart and you confess with your mouth you will be saved. You can lead many people to Jesus by leading them in the sinner's prayer. Lead them in a prayer to confess their sins and to open their heart to Jesus Christ. When you lead people to Christ, you have accomplished a great thing.

2. **Attempt great things by attempting to preach! You can preach the gospel of Jesus Christ to many lost and dying souls.**

And he said unto them, Let us go into the next towns, that I may preach there also: for therefore came I forth.

Mark 1:38

When you use your tongue to preach, you will save sinners from going to hell. Why don't you attempt great things for God by attempting to become a preacher? How can you live your life on this earth without ever preaching? How can you live your life without ever attempting a great thing for God?

Let him know, that he which converteth the sinner from the error of his way shall save a soul from death, and shall hide a multitude of sins.

James 5:20

It is a very great thing to be a preacher. It is far greater than being a lawyer or a doctor. It is far better to be a preacher than a nurse, an architect, a teacher or an engineer. Preaching is the greatest job because it is the job that Jesus did. When He had the opportunity, Jesus left carpentry and went straight into preaching. There is greatness in the call to preach the gospel.

3. Attempt great things by attempting to teach! You can teach the word of God.

And they went into Capernaum; and straightway on the sabbath day he entered into the synagogue, and taught. And they were astonished at his doctrine: for he taught them as one that had authority, and not as the scribes. And there was in their synagogue a man with an unclean spirit; and he cried out, saying, Let us alone; what have we to do with thee, thou Jesus of Nazareth? Art thou come to destroy us? I know thee who thou art, the Holy One of God.

Mark 1:21-24

Jesus Christ went to places just to preach and to teach. Teaching is a very powerful thing. This is all that Jesus Christ did with His life. Demons shouted out when He taught the word of God. They shouted, "Let us alone." When you teach the word of God, demons are confronted, dismissed and driven out of people's lives. The greatest thing you could do is to open your mouth and help people by teaching the word of God. You will do great things through teaching. All my life has been spent teaching the word of God, as I am doing right now by writing this book.

4. Attempt great things by attempting to prophesy!

You can prophesy with your tongue. God will do great things through you if you yield your tongue to Him. He will use your mouth to speak prophetic words. The apostle Paul said that he wished that everybody would speak in tongues and prophesy. What a great thing it is for God to use you in prophecy.

> I would that ye all spake with tongues, but rather that ye prophesied: for greater is he that prophesieth than he that speaketh with tongues, except he interpret, that the church may receive edifying.
>
> 1 Corinthians 14:5

Consider the prophecies of Ezekiel. His prophecies caused shakings, stirrings and unbelievable events to take place. "So I prophesied as I was commanded: and as I prophesied, there was a noise, and behold a shaking, and the bones came together, bone to his bone. And when I beheld, lo, the sinews and the flesh came up upon them, and the skin covered them above: but there was no breath in them. Then said he unto me, Prophesy unto the wind, prophesy, son of man, and say to the wind, Thus saith the Lord God; Come from the four winds, O breath, and breathe upon these slain, that they may live. So I prophesied as he commanded me, and the breath came into them, and they lived, and stood up upon their feet, an exceeding great army" (Ezekiel 37:7-10). Many great things will take place as you prophecy and speak for God.

5. Attempt great things by attempting to move mountains!

You can move mountains with your tongue! A mountain is a problem that must be overcome. You can overcome great mountains and solve great problems by the words from your mouth. Positive confessions and faith words will change your life and the lives of many others.

For verily I say unto you, That whosoever shall say unto this mountain, Be thou removed, and be thou cast into the sea; and shall not doubt in his heart, but shall believe that those things which he saith shall come to pass; he shall have whatsoever he saith.

Mark 11:23

Preaching and Teaching Every Week

And he went into the temple, and began to cast out them that sold therein, and them that bought; Saying unto them, It is written, My house is the house of prayer: but ye have made it a den of thieves. And HE TAUGHT DAILY IN THE TEMPLE. But the chief priests and the scribes and the chief of the people sought to destroy him,

Luke 19:45-47

It is important that you attempt to preach more and more in your lifetime. Jesus Christ taught daily so you must not just preach and teach occasionally. Attempt great things for God. Attempt to become a regular preacher and teacher for Jesus Christ.

And Jesus answered and said unto them, Are ye come out, as against a thief, with swords and with staves to take me? I WAS DAILY WITH YOU IN THE TEMPLE TEACHING, and ye took me not: but the scriptures must be fulfilled.

Mark 14:48-49

Even on the day that Jesus was arrested, He pointed out to His captors that He was a regular teacher of the word of God. Indeed, Jesus Christ did not only teach monthly or weekly as I have already suggested. He taught daily! Attempt great things for God and become a regular preacher of the word. Attempt to preach and to teach for the rest of your life.

CHAPTER 9

Attempt Preaching in a Hundred Nations

THE PEOPLE WHICH SAT IN DARKNESS SAW GREAT LIGHT; and to them which sat in the region and shadow of death light is sprung up. From that time Jesus began to preach, and to say, repent: for the kingdom of heaven is at hand. And Jesus, walking by the sea of Galilee, saw two brethren, Simon called Peter, and Andrew his brother, casting a net into the sea: for they were fishers.

Matthew 4:16-18

ttempt to be a great light to great multitudes! You can be a light to great multitudes by preaching to them about Jesus Christ.

Attempt great things for God by attempting to be a great light to many people. Jesus Christ came as a light to the world. Through Jesus, the darkness that has covered the human race will be dispelled.

Human beings think that the universe revolves around them. Most people do not know God. Most human beings do not recognize the reality of the Creator. God so loved the world that He gave His only begotten son to die for this dark world (John 3:16). Jesus came into the world to save us (John 3:17). He came as a bright shining Light to our dark world.

Jesus Christ is now calling on us to be a light to the world. Let your light so shine that many will know about Jesus Christ and be saved. You must attempt to be a bright and shining light to the nations of the world.

The people who sat in darkness saw a great light! This great prophecy was fulfilled in the ministry of Jesus Christ. Isaiah spoke of a great light that would come to the world (Isaiah 9:1-2). Matthew recognized that the prophecy of Isaiah had been fulfilled in the ministry of Jesus Christ. How did Matthew know that this great light had appeared? Only a great light could touch the lives of such great multitudes.

The greater a light is, the more people are affected by it. When you become a great light, great multitudes will come to know God. Notice how great multitudes were affected by Jesus Christ. You will notice the phrase, "great multitudes" being repeated throughout the Gospels.

And they immediately left the ship and their father, and followed him. . .

And his fame went throughout all Syria: and they brought unto him all sick people that were taken with divers diseases and torments, and those which were possessed

42

with devils, and those which were lunatick, and those that had the palsy; and he healed them. And THERE FOLLOWED HIM GREAT MULTITUDES OF PEOPLE from Galilee, and from Decapolis, and from Jerusalem, and from Judaea, and from beyond Jordan.

Matthew 4:22, 24-25

AND GREAT MULTITUDES CAME UNTO HIM, having with them those that were lame, blind, dumb, maimed, and many others, and cast them down at Jesus' feet; and he healed them: Insomuch that the multitude wondered, when they saw the dumb to speak, the maimed to be whole, the lame to walk, and the blind to see: and they glorified the God of Israel.

Matthew 15:30-31

And he came down with them, and stood in the plain, and the company of his disciples, and A GREAT MULTITUDE OF PEOPLE OUT OF ALL JUDAEA AND JERUSALEM, and from the sea coast of Tyre and Sidon, which came to hear him, and to be healed of their diseases; And they that were vexed with unclean spirits: and they were healed. And the whole multitude sought to touch him: for there went virtue out of him, and healed them all.

Luke 6:17-19

You must aim for great multitudes. Do not be satisfied with small numbers any more.

God has ordained that great multitudes should come to God through your ministry. You are ordained to be a great light with great multitudes following.

Attempt to have great multitudes!

Attempt to have greater crusades!

Attempt to have greater outreach meetings!

Attempt to have a larger church!

Attempt to have great multitudes!

Great multitudes are your destiny! You are destined to have multitudes follow you because you have become a great light for God!

Go ye therefore, and teach ALL NATIONS, baptizing them in the name of the Father, and of the Son, and of the Holy Ghost: Teaching them to observe all things whatsoever I have commanded you: and, lo, I am with you alway, even unto the end of the world. Amen.

Matthew 28:19-20

1. **Attempt to minister in a hundred different nations because Jesus Christ told us to go into the nations.**

   Go ye therefore, and teach ALL NATIONS, baptizing them in the name of the Father, and of the Son, and of the Holy Ghost: Teaching them to observe all things whatsoever I have commanded you: and, lo, I am with you alway, even unto the end of the world. Amen.

   Matthew 28:19-20

   Jesus Christ did not tell us to go to one nation. Why not have a new vision for your life and attempt to minister in one hundred nations of the world? Great fruitfulness is going to come into your ministry as you go out to minister to many nations.

2. **Attempt great things for God: Attempt to fill a hundred nations with the word of God.** The earth will be filled with the knowledge of God.

   For THE EARTH SHALL BE FILLED WITH THE KNOWLEDGE of the glory of the Lord, as the waters cover the sea.

   Habakkuk 2:14

3. Attempt great things for God: Attempt to go to the islands with the word of God.

Hearken unto me, my people; and give ear unto me, O my nation: for a law shall proceed from me, and I will make my judgment to rest for a light of the people. My righteousness is near; my salvation is gone forth, and mine arms shall judge the people; THE ISLES SHALL WAIT UPON ME, and on mine arm shall they trust.

Isaiah 51:4-5

It is very difficult to go to islands. There are natural barriers that prevent cars, trains and human beings from going to islands. People who live on islands are also important to God. Attempt to go to the islands and preach the word of God. Attempt to be a great light to great multitudes.

CHAPTER 10

Attempt to Plant a Great Tree

Then said he, unto what is the kingdom of God like? And whereunto shall I resemble it? It is like a grain of mustard seed, which a man took, and cast into his garden; and it grew, AND WAXED A GREAT TREE; and the fowls of the air lodged in the branches of it.

Luke 13:18-19

Attempting to plant a great tree is attempting to do something great for God. It is one of the great things you can do for the Lord. Every great tree has taken many years to grow. It has survived being eaten by animals and being cut down by human beings. A great tree has survived many storms and many seasons. A great tree provides shade for many people. A great tree provides wood for many people. A great tree provides a resting place for many birds. A great tree is a great thing and to have planted a great tree is a great accomplishment. The word of God calls you a tree planted by the Lord.

> **To appoint unto them that mourn in Zion, to give unto them beauty for ashes, the oil of joy for mourning, the garment of praise for the spirit of heaviness; THAT THEY MIGHT BE CALLED TREES OF RIGHTEOUSNESS, the planting of the Lord, that he might be glorified.**

> **Isaiah 61:3**

Seven Ways to Plant a Great Tree

1. Leading someone to Christ is the planting of a great tree.

If someone you lead to Christ becomes established as a great Christian, it will be even more evident that you have planted a great tree. If your convert grows up to be a strong Christian who helps many others, you will see that you have planted a great tree.

2. Preaching the gospel is the planting of a great tree.

I have preached at many crusades and led many people to Christ. There were people from other religions who prayed with me and received Christ. Many of them could not openly join Christian churches because of their religious restrictions. I thank God that I have sown the seed and I believe that seed will work and we will see all those souls in heaven. A great seed has been planted and a great tree of souls will grow.

47

3. Establishing somebody in Christ is the planting of a great tree.

Many years ago, a Christian sister helped to establish me in Christ Jesus. She took me to a Christian programme, introduced me to a church and helped me to buy my first Bible. She then taught me how to have my quiet time and established me in a Christian fellowship. Indeed, the seeds that this Christian sister planted in my life have grown into this book that you are now reading. You will never know whom you are following up!

4. Training a pastor is the planting of a great tree.

When you raise up a great person in the ministry, you have planted a great seed and given birth to a great tree.

5. Sending a missionary is the planting of a great tree.

The church of God in Ghana was planted by Swiss missionaries. This church has become a mighty tree sheltering over seventy per cent of the population.

6. Giving somebody a book is the planting of a great tree.

A book by Kenneth Hagin was given to me many years ago and it transformed my life. It turned me into a tree that has provided shelter for many birds.

7. Planting a church in a city is the planting of a great tree of a ministry that will grow and become a shelter to many souls.

Many of the souls in the churches I have been involved with do not even know me. But I can see that they are being sheltered and pastored by shepherds who know them and love them. A church is a great tree. Attempt starting a church because Jesus is building His church and it will be successful.

Jesus asked us to teach people and to baptize them. It is important that we fulfil the Great Commission and start churches everywhere. Souls are won when churches are planted. Do not forget how to plant a great tree!

And I say also unto thee, that thou art Peter, and upon this rock I will build my church; and the gates of hell shall not prevail against it.

Matthew 16:18

CHAPTER 11

Attempt to Grow a Church

So the churches were strengthened in their faith and
GREW LARGER every day.

Acts 16:5 (NLT)

Attempt great things for God! Attempt growing a church because the church of God can grow if you nurture it. Achieving church growth is one of the most difficult things to do. Many pastors are not able to make their churches grow. Many pastors find it very difficult to grow beyond seventy members. There are very few churches that have a thousand real members sitting in church on a Sunday morning. The gates of hell are postured against the church. Demons keep coming out of the gates of hell to attack the advancing church. You must fight to achieve church growth. Let it be one of the great ambitions of your life. Achieving church growth is more difficult than becoming a medical doctor. Make church growth one of the ambitions of your life. You will accomplish it.

Attempt great things for God! Attempt to grow a church! Attempt to have a large church! Attempt to have over a thousand members! Your church can grow if the Holy Spirit is working through you. You can have many church members if you attempt great things for God.

Attempt to achieve church growth! You are destined to multiply. You are destined to be great! You shall not be few! You shall not be small! The prophecy is clear.

And out of them shall proceed thanksgiving and the voice of them that make merry: and I WILL MULTIPLY THEM, and THEY SHALL NOT BE FEW; I will also glorify them, and they shall not be small.

Jeremiah 30:19

How the Apostles Achieved Church Growth

1. **Attempt to achieve church growth to the level of three thousand members.**

   Then they that gladly received his word were baptized: and the same day there were added unto them about THREE THOUSAND SOULS.

   Acts 2:41

51

2. Attempt to achieve church growth to the level of five thousand members.

Howbeit many of them which heard the word believed; and the number of the men was about FIVE THOUSAND.

Acts 4:4

3. Attempt to achieve church growth until everything is multiplied.

And in those days, when THE NUMBER OF THE DISCIPLES WAS MULTIPLIED, there arose a murmuring of the Grecians against the Hebrews, because their widows were neglected in the daily ministration.

Acts 6:1

4. Attempt to achieve church growth until the whole city comes to the church.

And the next Sabbath day CAME ALMOST THE WHOLE CITY TOGETHER to hear the word of God.

Acts 13:44

CHAPTER 12

Attempt to Build
a Great House

Nevertheless the foundation of God standeth sure, having this seal, The Lord knoweth them that are his. And, Let every one that nameth the name of Christ depart from iniquity. BUT IN A GREAT HOUSE there are not only vessels of gold and of silver, but also of wood and of earth; and some to honour, and some to dishonour. If a man therefore purge himself from these, he shall be a vessel unto honour, sanctified, and meet for the master's use, and prepared unto every good work.

2 Timothy 2:19-21

A great house is a house with many vessels. A great house is a house with many pastors. A great house is a house with many leaders who are used by God. It is the many and varied vessels that make up a great house. In a great house there are vessels of gold, vessels of silver, vessels of wood and vessels of earth. In a great house there are vessels of honour and vessels of dishonour.

A great house is a church with many congregations. It is the many different congregations that make up a really great house. A great house is a church with many branches. A great house is a great church! A great house is a large church! A great house is a growing church! A great house is a church with a thousand branches!

A great house is a house with great variety! A great house is a house with many vessels - vessels of silver, vessels of gold and vessels of wood all mixed together. When you have a small house you may have only one type of vessel. You may have only plastic vessels or you may have only ceramic vessels. But in a large house there will also be vessels of gold and vessels of silver.

1. **Attempt building a great house by planting a thousand churches.**

   He that hath an ear, let him hear what the Spirit saith unto THE CHURCHES.

   Revelation 2:29

Jesus did not speak to one church but to a series of churches. Attempt building a great house by planting a thousand churches. Please take note that there were a series of churches in Judea, Galatia and Asia. No city had only one church. One church can never meet the needs of a city. A series of churches are always needed to meet the needs of the millions who need Jesus. One church can never meet the needs of the people. A series of churches are always needed to meet the needs of the people.

For ye, brethren, became followers of THE CHURCHES OF GOD WHICH IN JUDAEA are in Christ Jesus: for ye also have suffered like things of your own countrymen, even as they have of the Jews:

1 Thessalonians 2:14

Paul, an apostle, (not of men, neither by man, but by Jesus Christ, and God the Father, who raised him from the dead;) And all the brethren which are with me, unto THE CHURCHES OF GALATIA:

Galatians 1:1-2

John to the seven CHURCHES WHICH ARE IN ASIA: Grace be unto you, and peace, from him which is, and which was, and which is to come; and from the seven Spirits which are before his throne;

Revelation 1:4

2. Attempt building a great house by having people from different nations.

After this I beheld, and, lo, a great multitude, which no man could number, of ALL NATIONS, and kindreds, and people, and tongues, stood before the throne, and before the Lamb, clothed with white robes, and palms in their hands;

Revelation 7:9

Attempt building a great house by having people from different tribes. Attempt building a great house by having both the young and the old.

Attempt building a great house by having people of different colours. Attempt building a great house by having people of different social backgrounds.

Attempt building a great house by having the rich and the poor in one house.

Most churches are made up of only one type of person, coming from one country or race. It is not common to find black, white and other colours all mixed up in one church. Most churches are either white or black. There is usually very little crossover. In certain countries black and white people never interact.

The greater the house of God, the more variety there will be. Do not accept to have a church with only one tribe. Do not have a church with only westerners! Do not have a church with only northerners! Do not have a church with only easterners! Do not have a church with only southerners!

If your church has only old people, it is not a great church. A church with only old people will be finished soon. A church with only young people does not have the benefit of the wisdom of the old.

Build a great house by having a church for both the high and low in society. A great house has educated and uneducated people. A great house has cultured and uncultured people. A great house has international people as well as the local people.

Vessels of gold, vessels of silver, vessel of earth and vessels of wood are all found in a great house.

Do not have a church with only poor people! Do not have a church with only rich people! God loves the poor and God loves the rich. Build a great house! Build a big house! Build a house with many vessels!

CHAPTER 13

Attempt to Build a Church

BEHOLD, I BUILD AN HOUSE TO THE NAME OF THE LORD MY GOD, TO DEDICATE IT TO HIM, and to burn before him sweet incense, and for the continual shewbread, and for the burnt offerings morning and evening, on the sabbaths, and on the new moons, and on the solemn feasts of the Lord our God. This is an ordinance for ever to Israel. AND THE HOUSE WHICH I BUILD IS GREAT: for great is our God above all gods.

2 Chronicles 2:4-5

I made me GREAT WORKS; I builded me houses; I planted me vineyards:

Ecclesiastes 2:4

And the king commanded, and they brought GREAT STONES, costly stones, and hewed stones, to lay the foundation of the house.

1 Kings 5:17

olomon built a house for God. He said, "The house which I build is great!" Whenever you build the church you are building a great thing.

Solomon made great works. He gathered great stones from Tyre to build the foundation of the house of God. He was truly doing a great work with great stones. These great stones were used to build a great house for God. What a great accomplishment that was! Up till today, we speak of the great temple that Solomon built. It was truly a great effort by the young man to honour his God.

What about you? Are you going to attempt something great for God? Are you going to attempt to build a church in your lifetime?

You must attempt great things for God. One of the great things you must attempt for God is to build a church building. God wants a house for His people. The church is what God is building. Instead of building mansions you will never use, why not build the church of God? Why not build something for God! Decide to be a part of those who value the church of God.

Thou shalt arise, and have mercy upon Zion: for the time to favour her, yea, the set time, is come. For thy servants take pleasure in her stones, and favour the dust thereof.

Psalms 102:13-14

Look at this beautiful scripture. When the servants of God take pleasure in the stones of the church, God favours His people. God showed mercy to Zion because His servants were interested in the stones of the temple. You will notice how Solomon sought great stones to build the temple. Solomon clearly took pleasure in the stones of the house of God. It is time for you to take pleasure in building the church. You must rise up and take pleasure in laying foundations, buying blocks, buying metal trusses, roofing sheets, tiles, toilet bowls and cement for the house of God.

What a great honour it is to take pleasure in the stones of Zion! What a great pleasure it is to favour the dust of Zion! The cement that is used to build the church is the dust of Zion. Choose to pay for the dust of Zion rather than choosing to build something for yourself.

1. Attempt great things for God! Attempt to build a church in your lifetime.

Be like King David! David attempted to build a church for God and it really touched the Lord's heart. David never actually built the church but he was rewarded for attempting to do so. This is all that God wants from you; a heart to build his church.

And IT WAS IN THE HEART OF DAVID MY FATHER TO BUILD AN HOUSE FOR THE NAME OF THE LORD God of Israel. And the Lord said unto David my father, Whereas it was in thine heart to build an house unto my name, thou didst well that it was in thine heart. Nevertheless thou shalt not build the house; but thy son that shall come forth out of thy loins, he shall build the house unto my name.

1 Kings 8:17-19

2. Attempt great things for God! Attempt to build a church because that is what Solomon did.

Solomon is famous because of the church he built and not because of his own home. Solomon spent seven years building his own house. I am sure his house was really beautiful. However, we do not have much detail on it because it was not that important. What was important was the temple that he built. Three thousand years have passed and Solomon's temple is still important and still in the news. You must respect the church of God. It is God's house!

And Solomon determined to build an house for the name of the Lord, and an house for his kingdom. And Solomon told out threescore and ten thousand men to bear burdens, and fourscore thousand to hew in the mountain, and three thousand and six hundred to oversee them.

And Solomon sent to Huram the king of Tyre, saying, As thou didst deal with David my father, and didst send him cedars to build him an house to dwell therein, even so deal with me. Behold, I build an house to the name of the Lord my God, to dedicate it to him, and to burn before him sweet incense, and for the continual shewbread, and for the burnt offerings morning and evening, on the sabbaths, and on the new moons, and on the solemn feasts of the Lord our God. This is an ordinance for ever to Israel. AND THE HOUSE WHICH I BUILD IS GREAT: FOR GREAT IS OUR GOD ABOVE ALL GODS.

2 Chronicles 2:1-5

3. **Attempt great things for God! Attempt to build the church because that is what Jesus did.**

Jesus said, "I must be about my Father's business." (Luke 2:49). His business was to build his Father's house. Jesus said, "I will build my church and the gates of hell will not prevail against it."

And I say also unto thee, that thou art Peter, and upon this rock I will build my church; and the gates of hell shall not prevail against it.

Matthew 16:18

CHAPTER 14

Attempt to do Business in Great Waters

They that go down to the sea in ships, that do business in great waters; These see the works of the Lord, and his wonders in the deep.

Psalms 107:23-24

Doing business in great waters is a great thing.

Being a missionary is a great thing! Why are you not a missionary?

Doing business in great waters is missionary work. Doing business in great waters is going across the great oceans to do the work of God. It is those who cross the seas to go on missions who see the works of the Lord and His wonders in the deep.

Doing business in great waters speaks of winning souls in distant lands. You have to cross great waters to see the islands and the harvest they possess. You have to do business in great waters in order to see the great works of the Lord and His wonders in the deep. Most Christians do not want to attempt great things. It is a great thing to attempt to work for God in great waters.

1. **Attempt to do business in great waters by going on a mission! Jesus came on a mission to this earth.** We were His mission field. He came on a mission to a very dangerous group of creatures called human beings. These human beings were full of wickedness, unforgiveness and revenge. Jesus attempted a great thing and succeeded. He succeeded in winning and saving millions of souls from hell. Jesus did business in great waters. It is now our turn to go on a mission!

After this, Jesus knowing that all things were now accomplished, that the scripture might be fulfilled, saith, I thirst. Now there was set a vessel full of vinegar: and they filled a spunge with vinegar, and put it upon hyssop, and put it to his mouth. When Jesus therefore had received the vinegar, he said, It is finished: and he bowed his head, and gave up the ghost.

John 19:28-30

2. **Attempt to do business in great waters by going on a mission. Paul did business in great waters. He attempted a first mission and crossed many waters to accomplish it. His first mission was described in the thirteenth chapter of Acts of the Apostles.**

So they, being sent forth by the Holy Ghost, departed unto Seleucia; and from thence they sailed to Cyprus. And when they were at Salamis, they preached the word of God in the synagogues of the Jews: and they had also John to their minister. And when they had gone through the isle unto Paphos, they found a certain sorcerer, a false prophet, a Jew, whose name was Barjesus:

Acts 13:4-6

3. **Attempt to do business in great waters by going on a mission. Paul continued to do business in great waters. He attempted a second mission which is described in the sixteenth chapter of Acts.**

Then came he to Derbe and Lystra: and, behold, a certain disciple was there, named Timotheus, the son of a certain woman, which was a Jewess, and believed; but his father was a Greek: Which was well reported of by the brethren that were at Lystra and Iconium. Him would Paul have to go forth with him; and took and circumcised him because of the Jews which were in those quarters: for they knew all that his father was a Greek. And as they went through the cities, they delivered them the decrees for to keep, that were ordained of the apostles and elders which were at Jerusalem. And so were the churches established in the faith, and increased in number daily. Now when they had gone throughout Phrygia and the region of Galatia, and were forbidden of the Holy Ghost to preach the word in Asia,

Acts 16:1-6

4. **Attempt to do business in great waters by going on a mission. Paul never stopped doing business in great waters. He continued in missions till the end of his life. His third mission was described in the nineteenth chapter of Acts.**

And it came to pass, that, while Apollos was at Corinth, Paul having passed through the upper coasts came to Ephesus: and finding certain disciples,

Acts 19:1

CHAPTER 15

Attempt Sending Missionaries

Howbeit Jesus suffered him not, but saith unto him, GO HOME TO THY FRIENDS, and TELL THEM HOW GREAT THINGS THE LORD HATH DONE FOR THEE, and hath had compassion on thee. And he departed, and began to publish in Decapolis how great things Jesus had done for him: and all men did marvel.

Mark 5:19-20

S ending people is an important spiritual achievement. You must attempt great things by sending people into the world. You may train people, you may teach them the word of God, you may appoint them but you may never send them. Sending people is not as easy as it sounds.

Jesus sent the mad man of Gadara on a mission. The mad man of Gadara published the gospel in Decapolis (Decapolis means the ten cities). The mad man of Gadara published the gospel in ten cities. Ten cities heard the gospel because Jesus sent one person. Failing to send people is failing to obey the Great Commission.

Most pastors do not send anyone anywhere. Sending people is like giving money. It seems as if you are losing something when people are sent on a mission. Money is spent on them, resources are given away and the home church seems to have lost key players.

However, sending out missionaries is one of the most important things you can ever achieve for God. Today, few people send missionaries anywhere! The inability to send anyone is a reflection of the true state of the church. The church is so sick and weak that it has no one to send.

If an army were made up of ten thousand children, ten well-armed grown-up soldiers could easily defeat it. Unfortunately the church is full of spoilt children who want more money, more toffees, more games and more nice times in the Lord. There is no one to send anywhere. No one is tough enough. Everyone is in debt and seeking more money. Many pastors have never sent anybody anywhere. If someone happened to migrate to a country, they would encourage the person to start a fellowship, and perhaps a church. But that is different from sending missionaries.

It is time to be more like Jesus Christ. It is time for the church to be more Christ-like. Why do you not send anyone anywhere? It is a great thing to send people. It is very godly, very anointed and very spiritual to send people. God the Father, God the Son and God the Holy Spirit are united in their desire and practice of sending people. It is very unlike God and unlike the Holy Spirit not to send people on a mission.

1. **Attempt great things for God: The Father sent Jesus Christ to this world.** Attempt sending people out to do the work of God because that is what the Father did.

    Then said Jesus to them again, Peace be unto you: as my Father hath sent me, even so send I you.

    John 20:21

2. **Attempt great things for God: Jesus Christ sent His apostles into the world.** Attempt sending people out to do the work of God because that is what Jesus did.

    As thou hast sent me into the world, even so have I also sent them into the world.

    John 17:18

3. **Attempt great things for God: The Holy Ghost sent Paul and Barnabas into the world as missionaries.**

    Surely, the Holy Spirit is still working today. If you have the Holy Spirit, I am sure you will send people. If you have the spirit of the world you will not send anyone anywhere. *The spirit of the world is the spirit of selfishness and self-preservation.* Attempt sending people out to do the work of God because that is what the Holy Ghost does.

    Now there were in the church that was at Antioch certain prophets and teachers; as Barnabas, and Simeon that was called Niger, and Lucius of Cyrene, and Manaen, which had been brought up with Herod the tetrarch, and Saul. As they ministered to the Lord, and fasted, the Holy Ghost said, Separate me Barnabas and Saul for the work whereunto I have called them. And when they had fasted and prayed, and laid their hands on them, they sent them away. SO THEY, BEING SENT FORTH BY THE HOLY GHOST, departed unto Seleucia; and from thence they sailed to Cyprus.

    Acts 13:1-4

CHAPTER 16

Attempt Ordaining Pastors

After these things the Lord appointed other seventy also, and sent them two and two before his face into every city and place, whither he himself would come.

Luke 10:1

And He appointed twelve, so that they would be with Him and that He could send them out to preach,

Mark 3:14 (NASB)

Whatever Jesus did was a great thing! One of the things he did was to appoint pastors and ordain disciples. In the middle of His ministry, He ordained twelve very young apostles.

One of your greatest spiritual achievements will be to train pastors and release them to work for God. It is all well and good to become a pastor yourself.

Training pastors is a higher calling. To achieve great growth in a church, you need to invest in pastors and not just church members. To achieve great growth in the ministry, you cannot just invest in your biological family.

If you want growth, invest in members! If you want growth, invest in your biological family. But if you want explosive growth, invest in ordaining pastors! Attempt training pastors because Jesus Christ trained His ministers. When Jesus no more walked openly among the Jews, He was mostly with His disciples. Most of the things we read in the book of John are from the training of His disciples. Attempt training pastors because Paul trained Timothy and Titus. Paul's letters to Timothy were his personal pastoral training to him.

1. **Attempt appointing and ordaining many pastors and elders.** Ordaining pastors sets the church in order. Ordaining pastors establishes great authority in the church. Ordaining pastors fills in great gaps in the spirit.

   For this cause left I thee in Crete, that thou shouldest SET IN ORDER THE THINGS THAT ARE WANTING, and ordain elders in every city, as I had appointed thee:

   Titus 1:5

Training pastors is different from graduating them, appointing them and ordaining them. All forms of human appointment will be fraught with error but the appointment of pastors is too important to ignore. The human errors that we make in appointing people as pastors cannot be compared to the benefits of people being appointed, ordained and authorized as ministers.

One of your great achievements in the ministry is to appoint and ordain people to the ministry. Aimee Semple-McPherson was the founder of the Foursquare Gospel Church. I always remember one fact about her ministry. She ordained many people into the ministry!

At the time she died, she had graduated eight thousand pastors from her Bible school. At her funeral, apart from other guests, one thousand seven hundred ministers whom she had ordained lined up in the cemetery to witness her burial. Even though over sixty thousand people paid their respect to her over three and a half days, the number of ordained ministers who attended the funeral did not escape notice.

2. **Attempt ordaining many pastors because it enables more people to preach.** Jesus ordained people so that they could be with him and eventually go out preaching.

   And he ordained twelve, that they should be with him, and THAT HE MIGHT SEND THEM FORTH TO PREACH,

   Mark 3:14

3. **Attempt ordaining pastors because that is what Jesus did.** Jesus believed in appointing and ordaining people. He was not content with ordaining twelve people. In His short ministry, he ordained at least eighty-two people.

   After these things THE LORD APPOINTED OTHER SEVENTY ALSO, and sent them two and two before his face into every city and place, whither he himself would come.

   Luke 10:1

4. **Attempt ordaining pastors because apostle Paul achieved great things by ordaining many pastors and elders in many cities.**

   And when they had preached the gospel to that city, and had taught many, they returned again to Lystra, and to Iconium, and Antioch, Confirming the souls of the disciples, and exhorting them to continue in the faith, and that we must through much tribulation enter into the kingdom of God.

And when THEY HAD ORDAINED THEM ELDERS IN EVERY CHURCH, and had prayed with fasting, they commended them to the Lord, on whom they believed.

Acts 14:21-23

5. **Attempt ordaining pastors because Titus was asked to ordain elders. Titus accomplished great things for God by ordaining elders in every city.**

For this cause left I thee in Crete, that thou shouldest set in order the things that are wanting, and ORDAIN ELDERS IN EVERY CITY, as I had appointed thee:

Titus 1:5

CHAPTER 17

Attempt Winning Souls for Jesus

Then said he unto him, A CERTAIN MAN MADE A GREAT SUPPER, and bade many: And sent his servant at supper time to say to them that were bidden, Come; for all things are now ready. And they all with one consent began to make excuse. The first said unto him, I have bought a piece of ground, and I must needs go and see it: I pray thee have me excused. And another said, I have bought five yoke of oxen, and I go to prove them: I pray thee have me excused. And another said, I have married a wife, and therefore I cannot come. So that servant came, and shewed his lord these things. Then the master of the house being angry said to his servant, Go out quickly into the streets and lanes of the city, and bring in hither the poor, and the maimed, and the halt, and the blind. And the servant said, Lord, it is done as thou hast commanded, and yet there is room. And the lord said unto the servant, Go out into the highways and hedges, and compel (ANAGKAZO) them to come in, that my house may be filled. For I say unto you, that none of those men which were bidden shall taste of my supper.

Luke 14:16-24

W e must attempt to win the lost at any cost! We must attempt to bring many people to Jesus.

Jesus has sent us out to witness for Him. Witnessing to the whole world is something we must attempt to do. We cannot sit down and do nothing! We must do great things for Jesus. There are many prophecies that tell us that we will be used to save people's lives. You are ordained to be a savior of men.

And saviours shall come up on mount Zion to judge the mount of Esau; and the kingdom shall be the LORD's.

Obadiah 1:21

This story is the foundation of all missions and missionaries. It shows how a certain man made a great supper but those nearby would not come. He had to rise up and go to the streets, the highways and the hedges, way beyond his normal circles. Every mission is borne out of a need to go beyond your circle of life.

A certain man did a great thing and the great thing he did was to make a great supper.

This great supper speaks of the great feast of the Lord that we are to organise to win the souls of men.

This great supper can be likened to organising a great church, a great crusade, a great conference, a great convention or a great Christian event. In eternity, we will be invited to the supper of the Lamb. Here on earth, we are expected to make great feasts and invite many people.

Having a great supper is to attempt great things for God. It is to attempt to go further and further beyond your colleagues, your friends, your country and your family. It is to go to the ends of the world, overcoming all obstacles and excuses. It is to travel away from your country and to go to people you would otherwise never meet in this life.

Why it is a Great Thing to Have a Great Supper

1. It is a great thing to have a great supper because you must give out many invitations.

It is not easy to give out many invitations. It is much easier to invite a few people. Without many invitations you will have a small feast. God has called us to do great things. We must aim to organise greater churches, greater crusades and greater Christian events by inviting many people. Sending out many invitations to many people is the number one challenge for someone who wants to do great things. Learn how to turn your church into an inviting machine. Make your members into great inviters of people.

2. It is a great thing to have a great supper because you must organize a lot of delicious meals for many people.

When people are invited to the table of the Lord, they must experience the greatest meal of all. At a great supper, there must be food and drinks for everyone.

At this great supper, you will have some bread which is the Bread of Life, Jesus Christ Himself.

At this great supper, you will have some meat which is the strong meat of the Word.

At this great supper, you will have fruits which are the fruits of the spirit.

At this great supper, you will have the living waters which is Jesus Christ Himself.

At this great supper, you will have the wine which is the blood of Jesus.

At this great supper, you will have a glass of milk which is the Word that you need to grow.

3. **It is a great thing to have a great supper because you must overcome many excuses of many people.**

The man who made the great supper encountered the three common excuses for not serving God: Work, Wealth and Wife. These three reasons prevent most people who are invited from coming to the Lord. Overcoming excuses is an art in itself, and without the ability to overcome the excuses that human beings give, you will never achieve great things for God. William Carey, the great missionary to India, overcame all these excuses in order to make a great supper for the people of India.

4. **It is a great thing to have a great supper because you will need to humble yourself to invite people.**

This man humbled himself and invited people from the streets, the highways and the hedges. He went beyond his normal circles of life and used the principle of *Anagkazo*[1] to achieve a great thing for God. Without *Anagkazo*, you cannot achieve great things for God. *Anagkazo* means to compel, to necessitate, to drive, force and to use all means available to bring people to Christ. Today, the world uses the principle of Anagkazo to get people to do self-destructive acts like drinking, smoking and gambling.

It is time to rise up and shamelessly do the work of God.

[1.] For further study, see the book *"Anagkazo - Compelling Power!"* by this author.

CHAPTER 18

Attempt Reaping the Harvest

After these things the Lord appointed other seventy also, and sent them two and two before his face into every city and place, whither he himself would come. Therefore said he unto them, THE HARVEST TRULY IS GREAT, but the labourers are few: pray ye therefore the Lord of the harvest, that he would send forth labourers into his harvest.

Luke 10:1-2

Jesus saith unto them, My meat is to do the will of him that sent me, and to finish his work. Say not ye, There are yet four months, and then cometh harvest? behold, I say unto you, Lift up your eyes, and LOOK ON THE FIELDS; FOR THEY ARE WHITE ALREADY TO HARVEST. And he that reapeth receiveth wages, and gathereth fruit unto life eternal: that both he that soweth and he that reapeth may rejoice together. And herein is that saying true, one soweth, and another reapeth. I sent you to reap that whereon ye bestowed no labour: other men laboured, and ye are entered into their labours.

John 4:34-38

Jesus spoke of the great harvest of souls that awaits believers today. Jesus said, "The harvest is truly great." There are over seven and a half billion souls in the world today. The harvest is truly great. We must reap this great harvest. We must attempt great things for God!

Do you want to attempt great things for God? Then get yourself involved in the great harvest that stands before us. Every nation in the world deserves the visit of an evangelist.

Every nation in this world deserves a crusade. Every community in this world deserves someone who goes house-to-house and door-to-door winning the lost.

Will you do something about the great harvest?

Today, churches are involved in great works. They are building schools, hospitals, banks, orphanages, universities and feeding centres. These are good things. But remember that none of these things actually saves souls. You will hear Christians say, "Prosperity with a purpose." I am happy with the idea of prosperity with a purpose. The purpose of prosperity is to win souls. However, there is very little soul-winning going on. Few ministries even do altar calls today. People live with dying souls all around them and do not care much for them.

Perhaps this is the greatest sign of the absence of the Holy Spirit in the lives of many ministries. When the Holy Spirit descended on the early church, there was a massive harvesting of souls. The large harvest began to be reaped when three thousand souls were added to the church. A few days after this five thousand souls were added to the church. At a point, the whole city came to hear the word of God.

Today, God is calling us to attempt to bring in the great harvest of souls. The need for harvesting of souls is greater now than has ever been. I am grateful to God for the schools you have built, I am grateful for the orphanages, the hospitals, the banks, the industries, the farms, the universities and the non-governmental organisations you have established. These are wonderful works.

But please turn your attention to the harvest! That is what Jesus said was a great work! The harvest!

Attempt Having Crusades

Then Philip went down to the city of Samaria, and preached Christ unto them.

Acts 8:5

Philip attempted great things for God. Philip attempted to bring in the harvest. He went down to Samaria and preached Christ. He was not from Samaria but he went there and attempted great things for the Lord.

Philip's crusade is reported for all time and for all eternity. It was a crusade Samaria never forgot. It was his first attempt at having crusades. Philip did it successfully. Attempt great things for God! Attempt to have great crusades! Attempt to bring in the harvest.

Attempt Having International Crusades

To PREACH THE GOSPEL IN THE REGIONS beyond you, and not to boast in another man's line of things made ready to our hand.

2 Corinthians 10:16

Attempt great things for God! Attempt to have crusades in the regions beyond. Attempt to have international crusades and bring in an international harvest. Attempt to be like Paul. Apostle Paul was not content to preach in one place. He was not content to keep going around in circles. He wanted to preach in the regions beyond. Having such a goal is what a man of God needs to do. Instead of thinking of how to build hotels and businesses, you must think of the regions beyond and what you can do for them.

The call of God is clear. The call of God is not the call to be a merchant man or a trader of silver, gold and other precious things. You must think of the regions beyond and how to reach other lands for Jesus.

Attempt Having a Thousand Crusades

Herein is my Father glorified, that ye bear much fruit; so shall ye be my disciples.

John 15:8

You can have "much" of everything. There is a higher level to the ministry that you have. You can do much more for God. Why not plan to have one hundred crusades in your lifetime? When you get to heaven, you will wish you had had a thousand crusades.

If you had twenty years of ministry, you could have had fifty weekly crusade nights every year. *Twenty years times fifty crusade nights is a thousand crusade nights.* Even Arts students can do this calculation. One day you will look back and wonder why you did not do more for the Lord. Why don't you attempt to have a thousand great crusades in your lifetime?

Attempt Crusades in the Islands

Attempt to go to the uttermost parts of the earth. Attempt great things for God! Attempt reaching the uttermost parts of the earth because Jesus said we should go to *the uttermost part of the earth.*

But ye shall receive power, after that the Holy Ghost is come upon you: and ye shall be witnesses unto me both in Jerusalem, and in all Judaea, and in Samaria, and unto the uttermost part of the earth.

Acts 1:8

Attempt to go to the ends of the earth. Attempt great things for God because Paul and Barnabas went boldly to *the ends of the earth* as a great example for us.

But when the Jews saw the multitudes, they were filled with envy, and spake against those things which were spoken by Paul, contradicting and blaspheming. Then Paul and Barnabas waxed bold, and said, It was necessary that the word of God should first have been spoken to you: but seeing ye put it from you, and judge yourselves unworthy of everlasting life, lo, we turn to the Gentiles. For so hath the Lord commanded us, saying, I HAVE SET THEE TO BE A LIGHT OF THE GENTILES, THAT THOU SHOULDEST BE FOR SALVATION UNTO THE ENDS OF THE EARTH.

Acts 13:45-47

Attempt to go to all the world. Attempt great things for God because Jesus prophesied that we will go to *the ends of the world* before He comes.

And this gospel of the kingdom shall be PREACHED IN ALL THE WORLD for a witness unto all nations; and then shall the end come.

Matthew 24:14

Attempt to reach the islands for Jesus. Attempt reaching the islands for Jesus! The islands are also the uttermost parts of the earth. Attempt great things for God because the prophets have declared that the islands will be reached with the glory of God. Islands are more difficult to reach. You have to cross the sea and reach people who are isolated and cut off. God has sent us to the islands as well. No one will be left out. Everyone will be reached with this beautiful gospel. The prophet Isaiah prophesied continuously about how the islands will be reached for God.

My righteousness is near; my salvation is gone forth, and mine arms shall judge the people; THE ISLES SHALL WAIT UPON ME, AND ON MINE ARM SHALL THEY TRUST.

Isaiah 51:5

SURELY THE ISLES SHALL WAIT FOR ME, and the ships of Tarshish first, to bring thy sons from far, their

80

silver and their gold with them, unto the name of the Lord thy God, and to the Holy One of Israel, because he hath glorified thee.

Isaiah 60:9

CHAPTER 19

Attempt Reaching Great Multitudes

And A GREAT MULTITUDE followed him, BECAUSE THEY SAW HIS MIRACLES which he did on them that were diseased.

John 6:2

ttempt to reach great multitudes by copying Jesus Christ. Great multitudes came to see Jesus! Why did multitudes come to Jesus? Multitudes came to Jesus because they saw His miracles! Multitudes came to hear and to be healed! Through the healing ministry, you will reach great multitudes. You are going to walk in the miracle power of God!

Attempt healing the sick because Jesus healed great multitudes of sick people. It is truly a great thing to be a channel of healing to people.

> And Jesus departed from thence, and came nigh unto the sea of Galilee; and went up into a mountain, and sat down there. And GREAT MULTITUDES CAME UNTO HIM, having with them those that were lame, blind, dumb, maimed, and many others, and cast them down at Jesus' feet; and he healed them: Insomuch that the multitude wondered, when they saw the dumb to speak, the maimed to be whole, the lame to walk, and the blind to see: and they glorified the God of Israel.

Matthew 15:29-31

Heal the sick because it was prophesied that Jesus would have healing in His wings. You must heal the sick because we are to do the work that Jesus did. What did Jesus do? He showed compassion! He ministered to the sick through the spirit of compassion. Jesus Christ is the fulfilment of the great prophecy in Malachi.

> But unto you that fear my name shall the Sun of righteousness arise with healing in his wings; and ye shall go forth, and grow up as calves of the stall.

Malachi 4:2

Jesus stands alone as the Great Prophet who came with healing in His wings. Jesus Christ stands alone as the One who showed such great compassion to many sick people.

Howbeit Jesus suffered him not, but saith unto him, Go home to thy friends, and tell them how great things the Lord hath done for thee, AND HATH HAD COMPASSION ON THEE. And he departed, and began to publish in Decapolis how great things Jesus had done for him: and all men did marvel.

Mark 5:19-20

You can attempt to do great things for God by attempting to set multitudes free from evil spirits, addictions and bondages. The mad man of Gadara had a great thing done for him. The mad man was healed through the healing ministry of Jesus Christ.

Jesus Christ did not get a job for this mad man. Jesus Christ did not pay the man's bills. Jesus Christ did not connect electricity to this man's house. Jesus Christ did not dig boreholes for this man to have running water in his village. Jesus Christ did not buy a ticket for this man to fly around the world.

Jesus Christ showed compassion to this man and set him free from thousands of evil spirits that had flooded his soul.

To set people free from evil spirits is to do a great work. To minister the compassion of Jesus is to do a great work. Attempt great things for God by ministering the compassion of Jesus Christ.

CHAPTER 20

Attempt to Have Great Gain

BUT GODLINESS WITH CONTENTMENT IS GREAT GAIN. For we brought nothing into this world, and it is certain we can carry nothing out. And having food and raiment let us be therewith content. But they that will be rich fall into temptation and a snare, and into many foolish and hurtful lusts, which drown men in destruction and perdition. For the love of money is the root of all evil: which while some coveted after, they have erred from the faith, and pierced themselves through with many sorrows. But thou, O man of God, flee these things; and follow after righteousness, godliness, faith, love, patience, meekness. Fight the good fight of faith, lay hold on eternal life, whereunto thou art also called, and hast professed a good profession before many witnesses.

1 Timothy 6:6-12

To be able to achieve great heights in ministry and remain content is indeed a great accomplishment. "Godliness with contentment is "great gain"! Attempt to achieve "great gain".

Our eternal judgment is going to be based on our faithfulness to God. "Well done, good and faithful servant!" These are the words we all want to hear. To be faithful means to be constant. Many are not able to stay on course. Many are not able to stay faithful because they are charmed by the riches of this world.

His lord said unto him, Well done, thou good and faithful servant: thou hast been faithful over a few things, I will make thee ruler over many things: enter thou into the joy of thy lord.

Matthew 25:21

To remain faithful is indeed a great achievement. Just as it is difficult for many men to be faithful to one woman, it is difficult for many ministers to be faithful to one God. Most ministers find themselves veering off into the love of money.

Attempt great things for God! Few of us are able to achieve a godly ministry and still be content. Few ministers of God are able to resist the temptation to become covetous. If you look around you will find that many "successful" ministries seem to emphasize on money, prosperity and "gain".

The "great gain" I am talking about is not the worldly gain of millions of dollars. The great gain I am talking about is "godliness with contentment". Worldly gain is different from spiritual gain. Godliness with contentment is great gain. Many are not content with material blessings that they are given by God. They want more and more. Many have shifted from real ministry into vain jangling.

Today, financial sermons replace sermons on Christian character and soul winning. God's word is turned into a manual for business, finance and worldly success. It is difficult to find men of God whose emphasis is not on gaining more and more financial wealth.

"Great gain" is the achievement of success in ministry with the spirit of contentment. To be happy with what you have financially, as you achieve your spiritual goals is indeed great gain. It is great gain because it is rare.

One day, a team of elders spoke to their pastor and said to him, "You are a great pastor and we have benefitted from your wonderful sermons through the years. Please stay in ministry and do not divert into business." But the pastor was bent on moving further into business deals on the side. These business deals ended up being a great scar on the ministry. Many ministers have not been able to escape the scourge of the financial deviation.

Indeed, it is difficult to find many of us who are able to stay on the road of great gain. Great gain is "ministry without covetousness"! Great gain is "ministry with contentment".

Great gain is ministry without greed! *Great gain is ministry without preaching constantly about money, prosperity, success and wealth.* Great gain is ministry with contentment. Great gain is ministering without imparting of the spirit of materialism.

Let us attempt great things for God. Let us aim at godliness with contentment. Let us believe the warnings that Jesus issued about money. Let us believe that it is more difficult for a rich man to enter into heaven than for a camel to enter the eye of a needle. Let us believe Jesus when He said, "Do not lay up treasures on earth but rather lay up treasures in heaven." (Matthew 6:19-20).

How to Achieve Godliness with Contentment

1. **Withdraw yourself from ministries that charge the congregation with a desire for money, materialism and worldliness.**

   Perverse disputings of men of corrupt minds, and destitute of the truth, SUPPOSING THAT GAIN IS GODLINESS: FROM SUCH WITHDRAW THYSELF.

   1 Timothy 6:5

Disconnect yourself from ministers and ministries that have taken on the mantle of covetousness and wealth-grasping. The Bible is clear that we are to withdraw ourselves from people who minister the spirit of covetousness. Gain is not godliness and godliness is not gain. From such withdraw yourself! There is no clearer instruction in the word of God.

2. Identify the spirit of covetousness in ministers.

And he said unto him, Went not mine heart with thee, when the man turned again from his chariot to meet thee? IS IT A TIME TO RECEIVE MONEY, and to receive garments, and oliveyards, and vineyards, and sheep, and oxen, and menservants, and maidservants? The leprosy therefore of Naaman shall cleave unto thee, and unto thy seed for ever. And he went out from his presence a leper as white as snow.

2 Kings 5:26-27

Covetousness is a spirit that seeks to receive many things that are not appropriate at the time. Gehazi had the spirit of covetousness and he needed to receive gifts and wealth that was not appropriate for the time. Elisha identified the spirit of covetousness in his protégé, Gehazi. Elisha actually rejected Gehazi because of the wealth-grasping spirit. Gehazi received a curse for desiring and receiving gifts inappropriately. This curse may also be available today for those who are desiring and receiving too many gifts.

3. Do not receive the leaven of covetousness.

In the mean time, when there were gathered together an innumerable multitude of people, insomuch that they trode one upon another, he began to say unto his disciples first of all, BEWARE YE OF THE LEAVEN OF THE PHARISEES, WHICH IS HYPOCRISY.

Luke 12:1

Do not think that listening to the wrong preaching will not harm you. Jesus taught us to beware of the leaven of the Pharisees, which was hypocrisy. Hypocrisy was the spirit behind the teachings of the Pharisees. Today, the spirit behind a lot of the teachings is not hypocrisy, but covetousness. Do you think that the Pharisees were teaching on the topic of hypocrisy? Do you think the Pharisees were teaching the people how to be hypocrites? Certainly not! They were teaching on good topics from the Bible but the spirit behind the teachings was the spirit of hypocrisy. Everyone who sat under their ministry became a hypocrite. Everyone who sat under their ministry became fake and unreal. Many things are spiritual. When you expose yourself to them you change without knowing what has happened to you.

You must be careful of the leaven of covetousness that is running wild in the church today. The leaven of covetousness is spreading like wildfire in the church. It is a spirit that is imparted by many top and famous ministries. No matter the topic these people preach, there is an impartation of wealth-grasping. Beware of the leaven of covetousness! That is the commonest leaven that is found in the body of Christ today.

4. Have a moderate lifestyle. Do not live an extravagant lifestyle.

But the fruit of the Spirit is love, joy, peace, longsuffering, gentleness, goodness, faith, meekness, TEMPERANCE: against such there is no law.

Galatians 5:22-23

Moderation is one of the fruits of the Holy Spirit. Another word for moderation is "temperance". Temperance is the art of doing things without excesses and extremes. Self-control and self-restraint of passions, appetites, and desires for wealth are very important in ministry. It is interesting that many of those who are constantly begging for money in church or on television actually need this money to finance extremely expensive lifestyles. Indeed, some ministers live as celebrities, film stars and billionaires. It takes a lot of money to finance these lifestyles and it is no wonder that we have many men of God who are constantly begging for money to pay their bills. The Holy Spirit will lead you on a road of temperance and you will not need to beg for money.

CHAPTER 21

Attempt Great Things: Attempt to Overcome Big Problems

And the angel that talked with me came again, and waked me, as a man that is wakened out of his sleep, ... And two olive trees by it, one upon the right side of the bowl, and the other upon the left side thereof... Then he answered and spake unto me, saying, This is the word of the Lord unto Zerubbabel, saying, Not by might, nor by power, but BY MY SPIRIT, saith the Lord of hosts. Who art thou, O GREAT MOUNTAIN? Before Zerubbabel thou shalt become a plain: and he shall bring forth the headstone thereof with shoutings, crying, Grace, grace unto it.

Zechariah 4:1, 3, 6-7

God has called you into this world to serve Him. Serving God is going to involve solving problems. A mountain always speaks of a problem. Mountains are problematic because they are difficult to climb. Indeed, some of them are impossible to climb! Some of the Swiss mountains I have been privileged to visit have very dangerous slopes with deep pits. Many people have disappeared into the deep crevices of these slopes. Some of these mountains have vertical rock faces that are impossible to climb. Many people have risked their lives trying to overcome the challenges that the mountains present. Every time you read of a mountain in the Bible, you must think of a problem. Mountains speak of great problems! Mountains speak of great challenges! Every call to the ministry is a call to solve a problem.

He that overcometh shall inherit all things; and I will be his God, and he shall be my son.

Revelation 21:7

As you can see from this scripture, you are rewarded because of what you overcome. You will be rewarded for overcoming the problems and challenges that confronted you on earth. Do not be too sad about the many problems you face! They will be the reason for the many rewards you will receive in heaven.

If you are called to the ministry in Africa, you are called to solve the problems in Africa. Do not complain about the problems in Africa. Open your heart and get to the job of solving the problems of ministry in Africa. The problems in Africa are financial problems, political instability, the lack of development, the lack of facilities, the lack of education, the lack of good leadership and the lack of resources. Instead of complaining about the problems in Africa, rise up and deal with them by the power of the Holy Spirit.

If you are called to the ministry in Europe, you will have to overcome the problems in Europe. The problems in Europe are pride, a lack of faith in God, a lack of the knowledge of God, humanism, prayerlessness, hostility to churches, immorality, homosexuality, a rejection of the existence of God, marginalisation of Christianity and the promotion of other religions to the exclusion of Christianity. Instead of complaining about the problems in Europe, rise up and deal with them by the power of the Holy Spirit.

Zerubbabel was faced with great and mighty challenges that prevented him from building the temple of God. He received a prophecy to be steadfast and to overcome by the anointing of the Holy Spirit.

The Spirit of God, the anointing of the Holy Spirit, is your master key to overcoming mountains. The Holy Spirit is the Spirit of wisdom. Through wisdom you can overcome impossible situations. The Holy Spirit is the Spirit of knowledge. Those who have the knowledge of science and medicine have overcome the problems that ignorant people grapple with.

The Holy Spirit is the Spirit of understanding. By understanding chemical reactions and biological facts, human beings have overcome amazing difficulties. Hearts, kidneys and livers are transplanted regularly all over the world. Lives are lengthened by wonder drugs that have come through the understanding of biological realities that God created.

The Spirit of God is the Spirit of power. When the Spirit of God is upon you, power lines up on your side and you become super human. Roadblocks are smashed and gates are broken through the Spirit of power.

The Holy Spirit is the Spirit of love. Human beings struggle to experience love. Broken relationships are the cause of most heartbreaks and disappointments. Through the Holy Spirit, love is restored. The ability to relate with other people is made possible. Marriage is possible because of the Spirit of love.

Today, the Spirit of God is working through you to move mountains. Trust in the Holy Spirit for grace to move mountains. It is the mighty Holy Spirit that we need. That is why we must minister the Holy Spirit every day.

References

Chapter 20

"*A More Excellent Way: Be in Health*", Henry W. Wright
https://books.google.co.uk/books?isbn=1603742026